Hello Kitty®
Papier-mâché
Activity Book

by **Mary Walsh-Kezele**

Scholastic Inc.

New York Toronto London Auckland Sydney
Mexico City New Delhi Hong Kong Buenos Aires

Illustrations: Yancey Labat

Thanks to Creativity for Kids (a Faber-Castell Company) for our author, Mary Walsh-Kezele.

ISBN 0-439-32843-8

12 11 10 9 8 7 6 5 4 3 2 1   2 3 4 5 6/1

Printed in the U.S.A.
First Scholastic printing, May 2002

Table of Contents

It's Time for Hello Kitty Papier-mâché

Welcome to another craft-making adventure with your favorite pal, Hello Kitty. This time, she has invited one of her favorite friends, Joey, to join in the fun. Together, this totally terrific twosome will show you how to make the best papier-mâché crafts ever!

Along with these fun-to-follow projects, you also get papier-mâché paper strips, papier-mâché glue, and a set of cool Hello Kitty paint pots and paintbrush! So, get ready to roll up your sleeves and experience the fun of papier-mâché!

Terrific Tips and Techniques

Papier-mâché is a French word that means "chewed paper." You can pronounce it like the French do: "pap-ee-ay ma-shay," or you can just say "paper mashay." However you pronounce it, crafting with papier-mâché is fun! All you do is combine paper, papier-mâché glue, and water. Once your project is dry, you can decorate it with paint (using the paint pots you received with this book), or with any other materials you like.

Papier-mâché Basics:

Most papier-mâché art is created using a mixture of glue and water to hold paper together. Here are the basic techniques:

Papier-mâché Solution:

For almost every craft in this book, you'll need papier-mâché solution. Why not make up a batch now, and save it to use on all your projects? All you do is mix one part water with one part glue. Keep any unused solution in the refrigerator and use it within two to three days. If you run out of papier-mâché glue, see the recipe on page 41 to whip up some more!

Here's a list of some of the extras you'll need to complete the projects in this book:

- Bowl
- Water
- Scissors
- Paper (newspaper, magazines, wrapping paper, paper bags, tissue, napkins, colored paper)
- Egg carton
- Toilet tissue tubes and toilet tissue paper
- Rubber bands

- Thin cardboard (such as cut-up cereal boxes or old file folders)
- Paper plates
- Aluminum foil
- Ribbon
- Yarn
- Plastic sandwich or bread bags
- Plastic garbage bags
- Round balloons
- Tape

- Flour
- Salt
- Spoon or stirring stick
- Wire coat hanger
- Stapler
- Shoe box
- Crayons or markers
- Assorted decorative materials (string, rhinestones, pipe cleaners)

Basic Form:

The easiest way to make a papier-mâché craft is to use a form as the base for your project. The form can be anything from a balloon to scrunched-up newspaper to a ball of aluminum foil. You can also use a *combination* of scrunched-up newspaper and foil to create your form. Once you've molded your

form into the shape you want, you're ready to begin layering on the papier-mâché. Some papier-mâché projects will take a little bit of paper, and some may take a lot. Start saving your newspapers so you have plenty to work with.

Layering:

Once you've made your papier-mâché solution and your basic form, you can begin layering by dipping the paper strips provided in your Hello Kitty papier-mâché kit into the solution and layering them over your form. When you run out of paper strips, you can tear up pieces of newspaper instead. Paste on as many layers as you like—the more you put on, the sturdier the project will be. To keep the surface of your papier-mâché project smooth, flatten out any bumps as the project dries. Seal any raised edges with a little extra glue.

Final Color:

Once your papier-mâché project has fully dried, it's ready to be decorated. You can use your paint set to give your project its final color (this could use up a lot of paint though, so try to save your paint for the finishing touches). Or you can add a final layer of

colored paper to your project for a pretty look. Just tear up strips of colored paper, dip them in the papier-mâché solution, and stick them on your project.

Découpage:

To make a project extra-special, you can add a final layer with designs cut from wrapping paper or magazines. Place the wrapping paper or magazine page on your project and paint over it with the papier-mâché solution to hold it in place.

Terrific Tips:

✓ Working with papier-mâché can get messy, so wear old clothes and cover your work area with newspaper or a plastic drop cloth. (To make a drop cloth, cut open one side and the bottom of a garbage bag, then spread it over your work area.) To clean up in a hurry, just gather up the plastic and throw it all away!

✓ Papier-mâché projects can take a while to dry—at least a day. If the papier-mâché feels cool, that means it's still damp. To speed up the drying time, place your project in a warm spot—like a sunny window. Turn the papier-mâché occasionally so that it dries evenly on all sides.

✓ Adding additional layers of papier-mâché will make your projects strong and sturdy.

✓ Your papier-mâché glue can also be used like regular glue. You can use it on your projects to glue pieces together.

✓ Some of the projects tell you to use "paper putty". This is an easy-to-make mixture (see page 40) that can be molded into any fun shape you like.

✓ If you run out of paint, you can decorate your creations with colored paper or markers, and craft materials like feathers or pipe cleaners are always fun to add.

✓ If you want to create new colors of paint, simply mix two different colors together to get a third color. Just follow the color wheel (right):

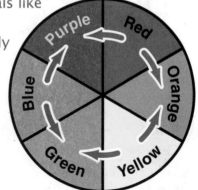

Blue + Red = Purple;
Blue + Yellow = Green;
Red + Yellow = Orange.

Hello Kitty's Birthday Party Fun

Birthdays are everyone's favorite special day!
Here are some great ideas from our favorite party planner, Hello Kitty!

Bangle Bracelet:

Hello Kitty and Joey love to make these cute bands for party gifts.

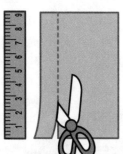

What You Do:

1. With a pencil and ruler, measure a strip of cardboard 9" long by 1½" wide.

2. Cut it out and bend it into a circle to form your bracelet. Overlap the ends and tape them together. (Adjust the bracelet as needed. It should easily slide on and off your wrist.)

What You Need:

- Pencil
- Ruler
- Thin cardboard
- Scissors
- Tape
- Newspaper
- Paper strips or newspaper
- Papier-mâché solution (page 2)
- Paint pots
- Paintbrush
- Wrapping or colored paper (optional)

3. Roll up small pieces of newspaper and tape them around the cardboard bracelet. Make your bracelet shape as thin or thick as you like.

4. Dip the paper strips (or strips of newspaper) into the papier-mâché solution and cover the bracelet. Use two or three layers of papier-mâché to make your bracelet sturdy.

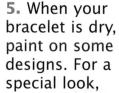

5. When your bracelet is dry, paint on some designs. For a special look,

use wrapping or colored paper and cover it, using découpage (see page 4).

HELLO KITTY SAYS

Wrap up your bangle bracelets with some pretty wrapping paper. Make a matching gift tag out of a small piece of folded paper (2"x2"). Decorate the paper with markers, crayons, or wrapping paper designs. Don't forget to write a special birthday message! When you're finished, attach it to your gift with a piece of tape.

Pretty Party Arrangement:

Hello Kitty—with Joey's help—likes to turn ordinary water bottles into beautiful vases and give them away as party gifts! Why don't you give it a try?

What You Do:

1. Use paper strips (or strips of newspaper) and papier-mâché solution to cover an empty plastic water bottle. Don't cover the top of the bottle.

2. Add paper putty or extra layers of papier-mâché to change the look of your bottle. Shape the paper putty or papier-mâché into stars, hearts, flowers, balloons— whatever you like! Press the shapes onto your vase, and allow them to dry. When the bottle is dry, decorate it using your paints.

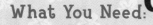

What You Need:

- **Paper strips or newspaper**
- **Papier-mâché solution (page 2)**
- **Empty plastic water bottle**
- **Paper putty (page 40)**
- **Paint pots**
- **Paintbrush**

Hello Kitty Piñata:

A piñata is a fun way to spice up a birthday party. It's a Mexican party favorite. You fill your piñata with candy or toys, put on a blindfold, and grab a stick. The first to break the piñata can grab as much candy as they want!

What You Do:

1. Inflate your balloon and tie it closed. Place the balloon in a bowl so that, as you work, it doesn't roll off the table.

2. Cover the balloon with paper strips (or strips of newspaper) and papier-mâché solution, turning it as you go. (But be sure *not* to cover the bowl.) Leave the top of the balloon uncovered. Make the opening large enough for your hand to fit through. (This is so you can remove the balloon later on and add treats to your piñata.)

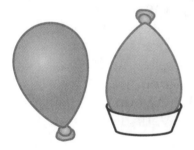

continued on next page

What You Need:

- Large round balloon
- Bowl
- Paper strips or newspaper
- Papier-mâché solution (page 2)
- String
- Scissors
- Tape
- Thin cardboard
- Tissue paper (or other colored paper)
- Ruler
- Pencil
- Glue
- Treats and trinkets

3. Cut a piece of string and tape it around the piñata, as shown. You will hang the piñata using this string.

4. When the first papier-mâché layer is dry, add another layer.

5. When your piñata is dry, it's time to decorate. To make your piñata look like Hello Kitty, cut triangle ears out of cardboard. Tape them to the top of the piñata.

6. Cut small squares of white tissue paper about 1" wide each. Pinch the center of each square, dip it in some glue, and begin covering your piñata.

7. How about a pretty bow for Hello Kitty? Use the pattern on page 43 to trace the bow onto a piece of cardboard. Cut out the bow. Then, as you did in step 6, glue squares of pink tissue paper onto the cardboard bow. Glue the finished bow over Hello Kitty's left ear.

8. Glue on black tissue paper for the eyes and whiskers, and yellow for Hello Kitty's nose.

9. Carefully cut the end off the balloon and pull it out.

10. Fill up the piñata with small treats, surprises, and candy.

HELLO KITTY SAYS
Grab a blindfold, a stick, and your friends, and take turns trying to break the piñata!

Party-favor Basket:

Fill up these cute party favor baskets with some candy or other treats at your next party!

What You Do:

1. Put some papier-mâché solution in a large, flat bowl. Dip a paper plate into the solution. Allow the solution to soak through the plate. Then place the wet plate over the bottom of a plastic container. Smooth and pleat around the plate until it lays flat against the plastic container.

2. Place a rubber band around the container to hold the wet plate in place as it dries.

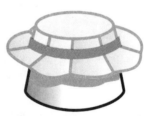

3. Bend back the wet edges of the plate to make a brim for your basket.

What You Need:

- Papier-mâché solution (page 2)
- Large, flat bowl
- Large paper plate (one for each guest)
- Small plastic container (like margarine tubs or deli containers, one for each guest)
- Rubber band
- Paint pots
- Paintbrush
- Tissue paper (optional)
- Scissors
- Colored paper
- Ruler
- Glue or tape

4. When the basket has dried, remove the rubber band and the plastic container.

5. Decorate the outside of the basket with your paints or tissue paper.

6. Cut three strips of colored paper (about 18" long each). Braid the paper to make a basket handle.

7. Glue or tape the ends of the handle to the inside of the basket.

HELLO KITTY SAYS
Another fun alternative to this party favor is to make the baskets out of printed paper plates that match your party theme.

13

Petite Party Cake:

This pretty cake looks almost good enough to eat!

What You Do:

1. Roll some paper putty into a ball. Flatten the paper putty between your hands to make a cylindrical cake shape scaled to the size of your Hello Kitty figure on pages 30–32.

2. Now make two more different-sized cakes—each one a little smaller than the last. Stack them on top of each other going from biggest on the bottom to smallest on top. Add a little glue between each layer to hold the layers together.

3. When the paper putty is completely dry, decorate the cake with paints or markers. If you like, write a message on top of your cake with a fine point marker. For a super-special look, sprinkle the wet paint with a little glitter.

What You Need:

- **Paper putty (page 40)**
- **Glue**
- **Paint pots**
- **Paintbrush**
- **Fine point markers or glitter (optional)**

e All Scream for Ice Cream!:

t's make some ice cream to go with our yummy cake!

hat You Do:

Roll some paper putty into a small pointed
cream cone shape.

2. Take some more putty and roll it into
a small ball—one ball for each scoop of
ice cream. Stick the ice-cream scoops
onto the cone while they're still wet to
hold them together.

3. When the paper putty is
completely dry, use your paints
to decorate your ice cream and
cone. If you like, you can sprinkle
the wet paint with glitter to make
sprinkles. Use a black marker to
draw lines onto your cone so it
looks real, if you like.

What You Need:

- **Paper putty (page 40)**
- **Paint pots**
- **Paintbrush**
- **Fine point markers
  or glitter (optional)**

HELLO KITTY SAYS
One scoop or two? Enough for me
and enough for you!

Birthday Balloon:

No party is complete without balloons! Did you know that you can make them out of papier-mâché?

What You Do:

1. Blow up a balloon and tie it closed.

2. Cut an 8" piece of ribbon or yarn. Fold it in half and tie the ends to make a loop. Glue or tape the loose ends of the ribbon or yarn to the top of the balloon so that you can hang it up.

3. Dip your paper strips (or pieces of newspaper) into your papier-mâché solution and lay them on the balloon. Don't cover the bottom part of your balloon so that you can remove it when you're finished.

4. When the papier-mâché is completely dry, you can paint your balloon or cover it with wrapping or tissue paper, using the découpage technique (see page 4).

What You Need:

- Balloon
- Scissors
- Ruler
- Ribbon or yarn
- Glue or tape
- Paper strips or newspaper
- Papier-mâché solution (page 2)
- Wrapping paper or tissue paper (optional)
- Paint pots
- Paintbrush
- Construction paper

5. When the paint is dry, use your paint to write "Happy Birthday."

6. Cut off the end of the balloon and pull it out.

7. To finish the bottom of your papier-mâché balloon, cut out a 2" circle of construction paper, as shown. Make a cut from the edge to the center of the circle.

8. Pull the ends toward each other until they overlap and create a cone. Tape or glue the cone in place.

9. Wrap a piece of long ribbon or yarn around the bottom of your balloon and glue it in place.

10. Hang up your party decoration using the loop at the top of the balloon.

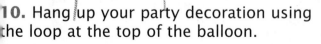

17

Hello Kitty at the Zoo

Come along with Hello Kitty—the papier-mâché
animal adventure is about to begin!

Dandy-Lion:

With the magic of papier-mâché, Hello Kitty and Joey can turn this fierce feline into a furry friend!

What You Do:

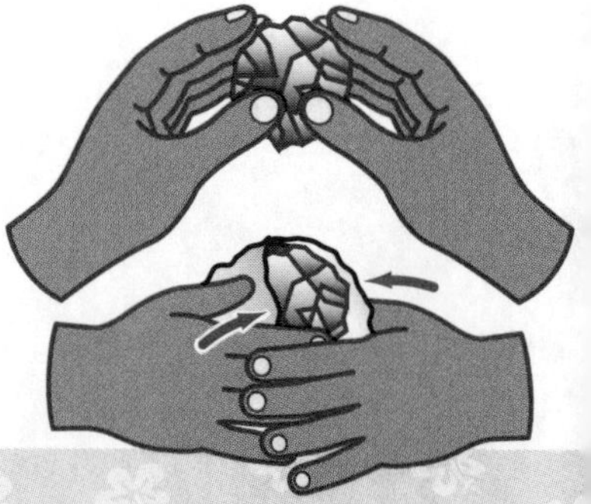

1. Roll some aluminum foil into a ball about 2" wide and cover it with a small sheet of newspaper.

What You Need:

- Aluminum foil
- Ruler
- Newspaper
- Tape
- Toilet tissue tube
- Scissors
- Thin cardboard
- Yellow construction paper (or paper strips or newspaper)
- Papier-mâché solution (page 2)
- Pencil
- Glue
- Paint pots
- Paintbrush
- Yarn

2. Tape it to the top end of the toilet tissue tube to make the head and body of your lion. Stuff the toilet tissue tube with newspaper.

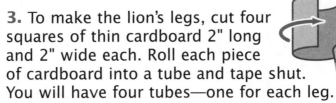

3. To make the lion's legs, cut four squares of thin cardboard 2" long and 2" wide each. Roll each piece of cardboard into a tube and tape shut. You will have four tubes—one for each leg.

4. To make the lion's paws, fold the bottom of each tube up, as shown. Tape the lion's legs to the bottom of its body so it will stand up.

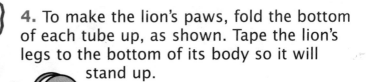

5. Use strips of yellow construction paper and papier-mâché solution to cover the lion. (If you don't have yellow paper, you can use paper strips or strips of newspaper, and then paint the lion yellow after it has dried.)

continued on next page

6. While the lion is drying, cut up several thin strips of yellow construction paper, about 2" long each (or use white paper and paint it yellow). Curl the ends of the paper around a pencil to make the lion's mane, and glue these around its face.

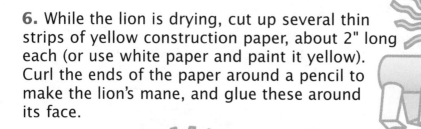

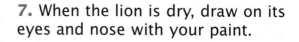

7. When the lion is dry, draw on its eyes and nose with your paint.

8. Glue a piece of yarn on to make the lion's tail. Pull apart the end of the tail so that it looks furry, just like a real lion's tail!

HELLO KITTY SAYS

You can make a leopard, too! Follow the instructions above, but instead of adding a mane, use a black marker or paint and cover your leopard with spots!

Huggable Hippo:

Hip, Hippo, Hurray for Hello Kitty's so-cute hippo!

What You Do:

1. To make the hippo's head, roll some newspaper into a ball about 3" wide.

2. To make the hippo's mouth, roll some newspaper into a flat, slightly puffy circle about 4" wide. Fold the circle in half. Attach the mouth to the hippo's head with some tape.

continued on next page

What You Need:

- Newspaper
- Ruler
- Tape
- Scissors
- Thin cardboard
- Gray construction paper
- Paper strips or newspaper
- Papier-mâché solution (page 2)
- Paper putty (page 40)
- Glue
- Paint pots
- Paintbrush
- Gray yarn or paper

21

3. To make the hippo's body, roll some newspaper into an oval 5" wide. Tape the head to the body.

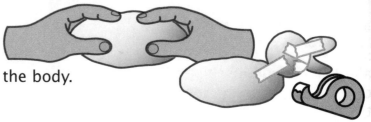

4. Cut four pieces of cardboard 1" by 3". Roll each piece into a tube and tape them shut. You will have four tubes—one for each leg.

5. Tape the hippo's legs to the bottom of its body so it can stand up.

6. Use pieces of gray construction paper and your papier-mâché solution to cover the hippo. (Or use your paper strips or pieces of newspaper, and paint the hippo gray after it has dried.)

7. Cut teardrop-shaped ears out of gray construction paper. Tape them to the top of the hippo's head.

8. To make the hippo's teeth, form some paper putty into two cylinders about ½" long each. When they are dry, glue them to the inside of the hippo's mouth.

9. When the hippo is dry, paint the inside of its mouth pink and its teeth white. Use black paint to make its eyes and nostrils.

10. To make the hippo's tail, cut a piece of gray yarn or paper about 3" long. Glue it in place.

HELLO KITTY SAYS
Did you know that hippopotamus is a Greek word, meaning "river horse"? Guess that's why you can usually find a hippo near water!

Cutie Turtle:

Don't hide in your shell, silly turtle! Hello Kitty and Joey are here to see you!

What You Do:

1. Using the patterns on page 42, trace the head, feet, and tail of your turtle onto a piece of cardboard and cut them out.

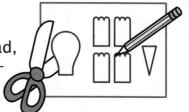

2. Glue your turtle's head, feet, and tail to the inside of one of the paper plates, as shown. They should stick out from the edge so you can see them. Let the glue dry.

3. To make the turtle's shell, take your two paper plates and place the second one facedown over the first. Staple halfway around the edges of the plates.

What You Need:

- Pencil
- Thin cardboard
- Scissors
- Glue
- Two large paper plates
- Stapler
- Newspaper
- Egg carton
- Paper strips or newspaper
- Papier-mâché solution (page 2)
- Paint pots
- Paintbrush
- Colored paper (optional)

4. Stuff crumpled newspaper between the plates. Staple the remaining edges together.

5. Cut out a bunch of egg carton cups and glue them to the back of your turtle to make a bumpy shell.

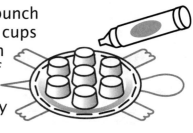

6. Use paper strips, or strips of newspaper, and your papier-mâché solution to cover your turtle completely. Be sure to cover its head, tail, and feet. Let dry.

7. Paint your turtle any color you like, or use some strips of colored paper and papier-mâché solution to put on a final layer.

25

Fanciful Fish:

Hello Kitty spies a school of fancy fish hiding in the seaweed!

What You Do:

1. Draw a fish shape on a brown paper bag like the one here. Cut out your fish going through *both* sides of the paper bag, so you have two pieces.

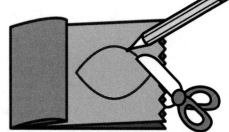

2. Tape or glue both sides of the fish together, leaving a small opening. (If you're using glue, let it dry.)

3. Stuff the fish with crumpled newspaper through the opening. When you're finished, the fish should look fat and puffy.

4. Seal the remaining opening with your tape or glue (let the glue dry).

What You Need:

- Pencil
- Brown paper bag
- Scissors
- Tape or glue
- Newspaper
- String
- Thin cardboard
- Paper strips or newspaper
- Papier-mâché solution (page 2)
- Paint pots
- Paintbrush
- Colored paper (optional)

5. Tape or glue a loop of string under and around the fish's body. This will be used to hang the fish up (since it can't stand on its own).

6. Cut fins and a tail out of cardboard, using the patterns on page 42 as a guide. Glue them to your fish.

7. Cover your fish with paper strips (or strips of newspaper) and papier-mâché solution.

8. Use paint to decorate your fish with fun designs, scales, stripes, or spots. Instead of paint, colored tissue paper and papier-mâché solution works great, too!

HELLO KITTY SAYS

When your fish is dry, find a special place to hang it up. You can even make a whole school of fish and hang them from your ceiling!

Bright Rainbow Snake:

This colorful wiggle worm is as friendly as can be!

What You Do:

1. Have an adult open up a wire hanger for you and bend it into a wiggly snake shape. If you don't have a coat hanger, a skinny, crooked stick will work, too.

2. Crumble and wrap dry newspaper around the wire or stick and tape it in place. Be sure to make the tail end a little skinnier than the rest of your snake's body.

3. To make the snake's mouth, roll some foil into a slightly puffy, flat circle. Fold the circle in half to finish the mouth shape. Tape the mouth to the body of the snake.

What You Need:

- **Thin wire coat hanger or a skinny, crooked stick**
- **Newspaper**
- **Tape**
- **Aluminum foil**
- **Paper strips or newspaper**
- **Papier-mâché solution (page 2)**
- **Paint pots or colored paper**
- **Paintbrush**
- **Scissors**
- **Thin cardboard**
- **Pencil**
- **Glue**
- **Styrofoam ball (optional)**

Dip paper strips (or strips newspaper) into the papier-mâché solution and wrap them around the snake. Cover the entire snake completely and set it aside to dry.

Decorate your snake with paint a fun rainbow pattern like the one here. If you don't want to use paint, use colored paper and your papier-mâché solution.

Cut and color a forked tongue out of cardboard, using the pattern on page 43 as a guide. Glue the tongue inside the snake's mouth. Paint on a pair of eyes, or cut a styrofoam ball in half and glue each side of it onto your snake. Then paint the eyes.

HELLO KITTY SAYS
You can make a sleeping snake, too! Bend the snake form into a coil shape, cover it with papier-mâché and then decorate it.

Hello Kitty and Her Friends

How would you like to make your own mini-models
of Hello Kitty and Joey?

Hello Kitty:

**Using papier-mâché and a few supplies, Hello Kitty becomes a work of
art. When the papier-mâché is dry, add a bow and paint on a perfect
Hello Kitty outfit!**

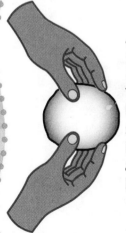

What You Do:

1. To create the
form for Hello
Kitty's head, roll
some newspaper
into an oval
about 5" wide
by 3" high.

2. Cut two small triangles
out of cardboard to make
Hello Kitty's ears—each
ear should be about ½"
tall. Tape them to the top
of Hello Kitty's head.

3. To make Hello Kitty's body, roll some newspaper into an oval shape about 3½" wide by 3" tall. Tape Hello Kitty's head to her body.

4. Use some more newspaper to make four small ovals about 1" long each. Tape these to Hello Kitty's body to make her arms and legs.

5. Dip paper strips (or strips of newspaper) into some papier-mâché solution. Layer the strips over the form until it's completely covered. Let it dry.

6. To put the finishing touches on Hello Kitty, tear up some white paper and dip it into the papier-mâché solution, and then cover Hello Kitty completely. Let Hello Kitty dry.

continued on next page

What You Need:

- Newspaper
- Ruler
- Cardboard
- Scissors
- Tape

- Paper strips
- Papier-mâché solution (page 2)
- White paper (about three 8½"x11" sheets)
- Pencil
- Paint pots

- Paintbrush
- Colored paper or wrapping paper (optional)
- Glue
- Sheet of black paper (or white paper and a black marker)

7. With a pencil, sketch Hello Kitty's eyes, nose, and mouth onto your Hello Kitty papier-mâché figure. Draw Hello Kitty a dress to wear, too (see page 43).

8. Use paints to color in your designs. Or you can use colored tissue paper or pretty wrapping paper and papier-mâché solution to make Hello Kitty's clothes.

9. To make Hello Kitty's bow, trace the pattern printed on page 43 onto your favorite color of paper and a piece of thin cardboard. Cut them out, then glue them together. Glue the bow over Hello Kitty's left ear.

10. Cut out three pairs of Hello Kitty whiskers (about 2" long each) from black paper, or you can paint a piece of white paper black. Glue the whiskers onto Hello Kitty's face—three on each side.

HELLO KITTY SAYS

Make my twin sister, Mimmy, and double the fun! Simply follow the papier-mâché instructions above for me and glue Mimmy's bow on her **right** side!

Pretty Purse:

Turn a little paper putty into a pretty purse for Hello Kitty!

What You Do:

1. Mold a small lump of paper putty into a little purse shape, like the one shown here. Make it small enough to fit in Hello Kitty's hand.

2. When Hello Kitty's purse is dry, decorate it with paint, wrapping paper, or markers.

3. To make the purse handle, cut a piece of ribbon or yarn and glue it to the top of Hello Kitty's purse, as shown. (If the purse handle seems too long, trim it with your scissors before you glue it in place.)

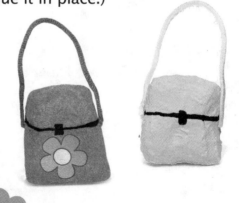

What You Need:

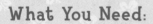

- Paper putty (page 40)
- Paint pots
- Paintbrush
- Wrapping paper or markers (optional)
- Scissors
- Ribbon or yarn
- Glue

Joey:

This cutie is the perfect papier-mâché pal for Hello Kitty.

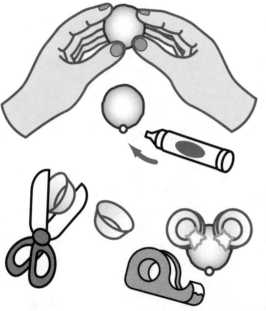

What You Do:

1. To make Joey's head, roll some newspaper into a 2" ball. Glue a tiny ball of paper at the end to make Joey's nose.

2. To make Joey's ears, cut two cups out of the egg carton. Trim the sides until they are roughly 1½" tall. Tape the ears to Joey's head.

What You Need:

- Newspaper
- Ruler
- Glue
- Scissors
- Egg carton

- Tape
- Paper strips
- Papier-mâché solution (page 2)
- Paint pots
- Paintbrush

- Blue paper (optional)
- Black pipe cleaner
- Paper clip
- Pencil
- 6" piece of yarn or string (black)

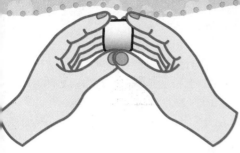

3. To make Joey's body, roll a piece of newspaper into a square about 1½"x1½".

4. Roll up two small ovals of newspaper to make Joey's arms (about 1" long each), and tape them to his body, as shown.

5. Dip the paper strips (or strips of news-paper) into the papier-mâché solution, and cover Joey. Let him dry.

6. Paint Joey blue or add a layer of blue strips of paper using the papier-mâché solution and let him dry.

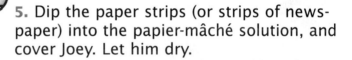

7. Paint a yellow circle in each of Joey's ears and add a dot of red paint or paper to cover Joey's nose.

8. Cut a black pipe cleaner in half. To make Joey's feet, bend the bottom of each piece, as shown here.

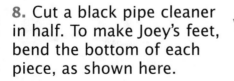

continued on next page

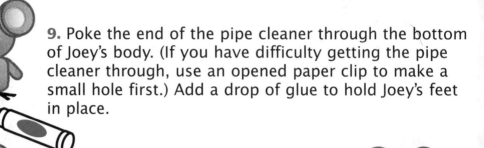

9. Poke the end of the pipe cleaner through the bottom of Joey's body. (If you have difficulty getting the pipe cleaner through, use an opened paper clip to make a small hole first.) Add a drop of glue to hold Joey's feet in place.

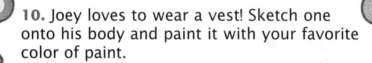

10. Joey loves to wear a vest! Sketch one onto his body and paint it with your favorite color of paint.

11. Paint Joey's two little round eyes on with black paint.

12. To make Joey's tail, glue a piece of yarn or string to his back.

Swiss Cheese, Please:

Let's make Joey his favorite tasty snack.

What You Do:

1. Squish a small lump of paper putty into a tiny triangle shape.

2. Let the triangle shape dry and then paint it yellow.

3. To make the clay look like Swiss cheese, paint little black or brown circles on it with your paint, or draw on the open circles with a black marker.

What You Need:

- **Paper putty (page 40)**
- **Paint pots**
- **Paintbrush**
- **Black marker (optional)**

37

HELLO KITTY SAYS
Making this cheese made me hungry. Why not create some other foods out of putty and make me some lunch?

Soccer Star:

Joey loves to play soccer with his friends. Use your paper putty to make Joey a miniature soccer ball.

What You Do:

1. Roll some paper putty into a small round ball scaled to the size of your Joey figure on pages 34–36. Set it aside to dry.

2. Paint the ball white, and let it dry.

3. Then use your black paint to draw a soccer-ball pattern onto the ball.

What You Need:

- Paper putty (page 40)
- Paint pots
- Paintbrush

Magnificent Mini-mirror:

Mirror, mirror on the wall, who's the most adorable friend of all? Hello Kitty, of course!

What You Do:

1. Squish some paper putty into a little flat oval with a handle, like the one on page 43. It should look like a miniature vanity mirror, scaled to the size of your Hello Kitty figure on pages 30–32.

2. When the mirror has dried, decorate it with your paints any way you like, or glue on some mini-decorations—like a ribbon, or a mini-flower made of paper putty, or maybe both!

3. To make the mirror, cut a small oval out of some aluminum foil. Glue it onto the mirror so that the shiny side faces out.

What You Need:

- Paper putty (page 40)
- Paint pots
- Paintbrush
- Ribbon (optional)
- Scissors
- Aluminum foil
- Glue

Hello Kitty
Papier-mâché Recipes

Paper Putty:

Paper putty can be used to add 3-D effects to your projects, or it can be molded into a fun shape like a soccer ball or a mirror. Whatever you like!

What You Do:

1. Tear up approximately 20 sheets of toilet tissue paper into tiny pieces. (Depending on the size of your project, add more or less toilet paper pieces, as needed.)

2. In a bowl, combine the tissue paper pieces with a spoonful of papier-mâché solution.

3. Stir together, adding small amounts of solution, as needed. The mixture should feel like soft modeling clay— not too wet, not too dry.

What You Need:

- **Toilet tissue paper**
- **Bowl**
- **Spoon**
- **Papier-mâché solution (page 2)**
- **Plastic bag**

4. Place the unused portion in a plastic bag and refrigerate. Use the paper putty within two to three days.

40

Papier-mâché Glue:

If you run out of papier-mâché glue, and there's no white glue in the house, don't worry! Use this recipe to mix up a batch of fresh papier-mâché glue.

What You Do:

1. In a bowl, mix together the salt, flour, and a half cup of water. Mix everything together with a fork to remove any lumps.

2. Slowly add the rest of the water (1½ cups). Continue stirring until smooth. The solution should feel like runny oatmeal. If it's too thick, add more water; if it's too thin, add a little extra flour.

3. Cover the bowl with plastic wrap, label the container, and place it in the refrigerator until you're ready to use it. The papier-mâché glue should be used within two to three days.

What You Need:

- Bowl
- 1 tablespoon salt
- 1 cup flour
- 2 cups warm water
- Fork
- Plastic wrap
- Label and pen

Hello Kitty
Shapes to Trace

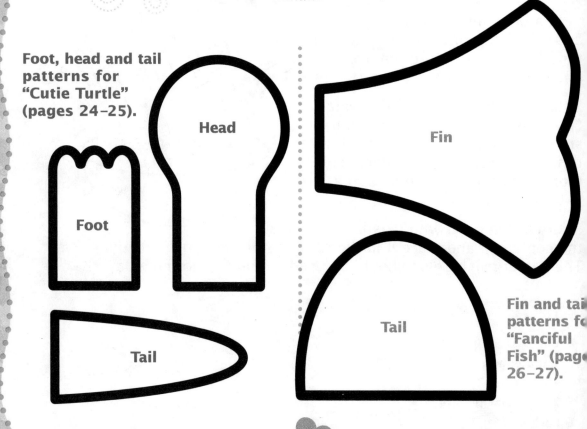

Foot, head and tail patterns for "Cutie Turtle" (pages 24–25).

Head

Foot

Tail

Fin

Tail

Fin and tail patterns for "Fanciful Fish" (pages 26–27).

Bow pattern for "Hello Kitty Piñata" (pages 9–11).

Dress and bow patterns for "Hello Kitty" (pages 30–32).

Tongue pattern for "Bright Rainbow Snake" (pages 28–29).

Pattern for "Magnificent Mini-mirror" (page 39).

Au revoir from Hello Kitty and Joey

The next time you're looking for something fun to do, gather up your pals, stir up some papier-mâché solution, and have a great time. Crafting and creating with friends is a great way to spend the day!

Thanks for coming along on our papier-mâché adventure. We hope these creative crafts have sparked your imagination. Great ideas are all around you, so keep your eyes and ears open. Until next time, remember to always be yourself and let your artistic personality shine through!

Many hugs, xoxox

Hello Kitty and Joey